The Duke of Gandia by Algernon Charles Swinburne

Algernon Charles Swinburne was born on April 5th, 1837, in London, into a wealthy Northumbrian family. He was educated at Eton and at Balliol College, Oxford, but did not complete a degree.

In 1860 Swinburne published two verse dramas but achieved his first literary success in 1865 with Atalanta in Calydon, written in the form of classical Greek tragedy. The following year "Poems and Ballads" brought him instant notoriety. He was now identified with "indecent" themes and the precept of art for art's sake.

Although he produced much after this success in general his popularity and critical reputation declined. The most important qualities of Swinburne's work are an intense lyricism, his intricately extended and evocative imagery, metrical virtuosity, rich use of assonance and alliteration, and bold, complex rhythms.

Swinburne's physical appearance was small, frail, and plagued by several other oddities of physique and temperament. Throughout the 1860s and 1870s he drank excessively and was prone to accidents that often left him bruised, bloody, or unconscious. Until his forties he suffered intermittent physical collapses that necessitated removal to his parents' home while he recovered.

Throughout his career Swinburne also published literary criticism of great worth. His deep knowledge of world literatures contributed to a critical style rich in quotation, allusion, and comparison. He is particularly noted for discerning studies of Elizabethan dramatists and of many English and French poets and novelists. As well he was a noted essayist and wrote two novels.

In 1879, Swinburne's friend and literary agent, Theodore Watts-Dunton, intervened during a time when Swinburne was dangerously ill. Watts-Dunton isolated Swinburne at a suburban home in Putney and gradually weaned him from alcohol, former companions and many other habits as well.

Much of his poetry in this period may be inferior but some individual poems are exceptional; "By the North Sea," "Evening on the Broads," "A Nympholept," "The Lake of Gaube," and "Neap-Tide."

Swinburne lived another thirty years with Watts-Dunton. He denied Swinburne's friends access to him, controlled the poet's money, and restricted his activities. It is often quoted that 'he saved the man but killed the poet'.

Swinburne died on April 10th, 1909 at the age of seventy-two.

Index of Contents

Scene IV
Algernon Charles Swinburne – A short Biography
Algernon Charles Swinburne – A Concise Bibliography

POPE ALEXANDER VI.
FRANCESCO BORGIA, Duke of Gandia   } his sons
CÆSAR BORGIA, Cardinal of Valencia   }
DON MICHELE COREGLIA, called MICHELOTTO, agent for Cæsar Borgia.
GIORGIO SCHIAVONE, a Tiber waterman.

TWO ASSASSINS.
AN OFFICER of the Papal Household.

VANNOZZA CATANEI, surnamed LA ROSA, concubine to the Pope.
LUCREZIA BORGIA, daughter to Alexander and Vannozza.

SCENE

ROME.

TIME

JUNE 14–JULY 22, 1497.

THE DUKE OF GANDIA

SCENE I

The Vatican

Enter **CÆSAR** and **VANNOZZA**

CÆSAR
Now, mother, though thou love my brother more,
Am I not more thy son than he?

VANNOZZA
Not more.

CÆSAR
Have I more Spaniard in me—less of thee?

Did our Most Holiest father thrill thy womb
With more Italian passion than brought forth
Me?

VANNOZZA
Child, thine elder never was as thou—
Spake never thus.

CÆSAR
I doubt it not. But I,
Mother, am not mine elder. He desires
And he enjoys the life God gives him—God,
The Pope our father, and thy sacred self,
Mother beloved and hallowed. I desire
More.

VANNOZZA
Thou wast ever sleepless as the wind—
A child anhungered for thy time to be
Man. See thy purple about thee. Art thou not
Cardinal?

CÆSAR
Ay; my father's eminence
Set so the stamp on mine. I will not die
Cardinal.

VANNOZZA
Cæsar, wilt thou cleave my heart?
Have I not loved thee?

CÆSAR
Ay, fair mother—ay.
Thou hast loved my father likewise. Dost thou love
Giulia—the sweet Farnese—called the Fair
In all the Roman streets that call thee Rose?
And that bright babe Giovanni, whom our sire,
Thy holy lord and hers, hath stamped at birth
As duke of Nepi?

VANNOZZA
When thy sire begat
Thee, sinful though he ever was—fierce, fell,
Spaniard—I fear me, Jesus for his sins
Bade Satan pass into him.

CÆSAR
And fill thee full,

Sweet sinless mother. Fear it not. Thou hast
Children more loved of him and thee than me—
Our bright Francesco, born to smile and sway,
And her whose face makes pale the sun in heaven,
Whose eyes outlaugh the splendour of the sea,
Whose hair has all noon's wonders in its weft,
Whose mouth is God's and Italy's one rose,
Lucrezia.

VANNOZZA
Dost thou love them then? My child,
How should not I then love thee?

CÆSAR
God alone
Knows. Was not God—the God of love, who bade
His son be man because he hated man,
And saw him scourged and hanging, and at last
Forgave the sin wherewith he had stamped us, seeing
So fair a full atonement—was not God
Bridesman when Christ's crowned vicar took to bride
My mother?

VANNOZZA
Speak not thou to me of God.
I have sinned, I have sinned—I would I had died a nun,
Cloistered!

CÆSAR
There too my sire had found thee. Priests
Make way where warriors dare not—save when war
Sets wide the floodgates of the weirs of hell.
And what hast thou to do with sin? Hath he
Whose sin was thine not given thee there and then
God's actual absolution? Mary lived
God's virgin, and God's mother: mine art thou,
Who am Christlike even as thou art virginal.
And if thou love me or love me not God knows,
And God, who made me and my sire and thee,
May take the charge upon him. I am I.
Somewhat I think to do before my day
Pass from me. Did I love thee not at all,
I would not bid thee know it.

VANNOZZA
Alas, my son!

CÆSAR

Alas, my mother, sounds no sense for men—
Rings but reverberate folly, whence resounds
Returning laughter. Weep or smile on me,
Thy sunshine or thy rainbow softens not
The mortal earth wherein thou hast clad me. Nay,
But rather would I see thee smile than weep,
Mother. Thou art lovelier, smiling.

VANNOZZA
What is this
Thou hast at heart to do? God's judgment hangs
Above us. I that girdled thee in me
As Mary girdled Jesus yet unborn
—Thou dost believe it? A creedless heretic
Thou art not?

CÆSAR
I? God's vicar's child?

VANNOZZA
Be God
Praised! I, then, I, thy mother, bid thee, pray,
Pray thee but say what hungers in thy heart,
And whither thou wouldst hurl the strenuous life
That works within thee.

CÆSAR
Whither? Am not I
Hinge of the gate that opens heaven—that bids
God open when my sire thrusts in the key—
Cardinal? Canst thou dream I had rather be
Duke?

[Enter **FRANCESCO**

FRANCESCO
Wilt thou take mine office, Cæsar mine?
I heard thy laugh deride it. Mother, whence
Comes that sweet gift of grace from dawn to dawn
That daily shows thee sweeter?

CÆSAR
Knowest thou none
Lovelier?

VANNOZZA
My Cæsar finds me not so fair.
Thou art over fond, Francesco.

CÆSAR
Nay, no whit.
Our heavenly father on earth adores no less
Our mother than our sister: and I hold
His heart and eye, his spirit and his sense,
Infallible.

[Enter **POPE ALEXANDER VI**

ALEXANDER
Jest not with God. I heard
A holy word, a hallowing epithet,
Cardinal Cæsar, trip across thy tongue
Lightly.

CÆSAR
Most holiest father, I desire
Paternal absolution—when thy laugh
Has waned from lip and eyelid.

ALEXANDER
Take it now,
And Christ preserve thee, Cæsar, as thou art,
To serve him as I serve him. Rose of mine,
My rose of roses, whence has fallen this dew
That dims the sweetest eyes love ever lit
With light that mocks the morning?

VANNOZZA
Nay, my lord,
I know not—nay, I knew not if I wept.

ALEXANDER
Our sons and Christ's and Peter's whom we praise,
Are they—are these—fallen out?

FRANCESCO
Not I with him,
Nor he, I think, with me.

CÆSAR
Forbid it, God!
The God that set thee where thou art, and there
Sustains thee, bids the love he kindles bind
Brother to brother.

ALEXANDER

God or no God, man
Must live and let man live—while one man's life
Galls not another's. Fools and fiends are men
Who play the fiend that is not. Why shouldst thou,
Girt with the girdle of the church, and given
Power to preside on spirit and flesh—or thou,
Clothed with the glad world's glory—priest or prince,
Turn on thy brother an evil eye, or deem
Your father God hath dealt his doom amiss
Toward either or toward any? Hath not Rome,
Hath not the Lord Christ's kingdom, where his will
Is done on earth, enough of all that man
Thirsts, hungers, lusts for—pleasure, pride, and power—
To sate you and to share between you? Whence
Should she, the godless heathen's goddess once,
Discord, heave up her hissing head again
Between love's Christian children—love's? Hath God
Cut short the thrill that glorifies the flesh,
Chilled the sharp rapturous pang that burns the blood,
Because an hundred even as twain at once
Partake it? Boys, my boys, be wise, and rest,
Whatever fire take hold upon your flesh,
Whatever dream set all your life on fire,
Friends.

CÆSAR
Friends? Our father on earth, thy will be done.

FRANCESCO
Christ's body, Cæsar! dost thou mock?

CÆSAR
Not I.
Hast thou fallen out with me, then, that thy tongue
Disclaims its lingering utterance?

ALEXANDER
Now, by nought,
As nought abides to swear by, folly seen
So plain and heard so loud might well nigh make
Wise men believe in even the devil and God.
What ails you? Whence comes lightning in your eyes,
With hissing hints of thunder on your lips?
Fools! and the fools I thought to make for men
Gods. Is it love or hate divides you—turns
Tooth, fang, or claw, when time provides them prey,
To nip, rip, rend each other?

CÆSAR
Hate or love,
Francesco?

FRANCESCO
Why, I hate thee not—thou knowest
I hate thee not, my Cæsar.

CÆSAR
I believe
Thou dost not hate or love or envy me;
Even as I know, and knowing believe, we all—
Our father, thou and I—triune in heart—
Hold loveliest of all living things to love
This.

[Enter **LUCREZIA**

LUCREZIA
Mother! What do tears and thou for once
Together? Rain in sunshine?

VANNOZZA
Ask thy sire,
Am I not now the moon? Saint Anna bore
Saint Mary Virgin—did not God prefer
The child, and thrust behind with scarce a smile
The mother?

ALEXANDER
Thrust not out thy thorns at heaven,
Rose.

LUCREZIA
But what ailed her? And she will not say.

CÆSAR
Sister, I sinned—sin must be mine. A word
Fell out askance between us, and she wept
Because our father chid us.

LUCREZIA
How should strife
Find here a tongue to hiss with? Are not we,
Brothers and sire and sister, sealed of God
Lovers—made one in love?

ALEXANDER

Deride not God,
Lucrezia.

LUCREZIA
Father, dost thou fear him, then?

ALEXANDER
I say not and I know not if I fear.

FRANCESCO
Thou canst not. Father, were he terrible,
How long wouldst thou live—thou, his mask on earth?

ALEXANDER
Boy, art thou all a child? What knew they more,
The men that loved and feared and died for God,
Than I and thou who know him not? We know
This life is ours, and sweet, if shame and fear
Make us not less than man: and less were they
Who crawled and writhed and cowered and called on God
To save them from him. Here I stand as he,
God, or God's very figure wrought in flesh,
More godlike than was Jesus. Dare I fear
Whipping and hanging? Thou, my cardinal,
Canst think not to be scourged and crucified—
Ha?

CÆSAR
Nay: there lurks no God in me. And thou,
Father, dost thou fear?

ALEXANDER
I? Nought less than God.
But if we take him lightly on our lips
Too light his name will sound in all men's ears
Till earth and air, when man says God, respond
Laughter. Forbear him.

CÆSAR
Wisdom lives in thee,
And cries not out along the streets as when
None of God's folk that heard regarded her,
As all that hear thy word regard—or die,
Being not outside God's eyeshot. Dost thou sleep
Here in his special keeping—here—to-night,
Brother?

FRANCESCO

What bids thee care to know?

CÆSAR
They say
These holy streets of heaven's most holiest choice
Lie dangerous now in darkness if a man
Walk not on holiest errands. Thou, they say,
Wert scarce a Christlike sacrifice if slain.
Too many dead flow down the Tiber's flow
Nightly. They say it.

FRANCESCO
I never called thee yet
Fool.

CÆSAR
Ah, my lord and brother, didst thou now,
Were this not thankless? God—our father's God—
Guide thee!

[Exit **FRANCESCO**.

He goes, and thanks me not. Our sire,
What says the God that lives upon thy lips
And withers in thy silence?

LUCREZIA
Vex him not,
Cæsar. Thou seest he is weary.

ALEXANDER
Yea. Come ye
With me. Bethink thee, Cæsar. Vex me not.

[Exeunt **ALEXANDER**, **VANNOZZA**, and **LUCREZIA**.

CÆSAR

Thou wilt not bid me this, I think, again,
Father.

[Enter **MICHELOTTO**

Thou art swift of speed at need. I bade thee
Abide my bidding.

MICHELOTTO
Till my lord were left

Alone.

CÆSAR
Thou knewest it?

MICHELOTTO
Where my lord may be
And what beseems his thrall to know of him
I were not worthy, knew I not, to know.

CÆSAR
I do not ask thee where my brother sleeps.
And where to-morrow sees him yet asleep—

MICHELOTTO
Ask of the fishers' nets on Tiber.

CÆSAR
Nay—
Not I but Rome shall ask it. Pass in peace.
The benediction of my sire be thine.

[Exeunt.

SCENE II

A narrow street opening on the Tiber

Enter **MICHELOTTO** and **ASSASSINS**

MICHELOTTO
Ye know the lordlier harlot's house—there?

FIRST ASSASSIN
Ay,
Surely.

MICHELOTTO
The first whose foot comes forth is he.

SECOND ASSASSIN
How know we this?

MICHELOTTO
I know it. Ye need but slay.

[Exit.

[Enter **FRANCESCO**

FRANCESCO [singing]
Love and night are life and light;
Sleep and wine and song
Speed and slay the halting day
Ere it live too long.

FIRST ASSASSIN
That shalt not thou. Sing, whosoe'er thou be,
Thy next of songs to Satan.

[They stab him.

FRANCESCO
Dogs! Ye dare?
God! Pity me! God!

[Dies.

SECOND ASSASSIN
God receive his soul!
This was a Christian: many a man I have slain
Died with all hell between his lips.

FIRST ASSASSIN
Be thine
Dumb. Lift his feet as I the head.

SECOND ASSASSIN
A boy!
And fair of face as angels

FIRST ASSASSIN
If the nets
Snare not this fish betimes ere others feed,
None that shall heave it airward for the sun
To mock and mar shall say so. Bring him down.
Tiber hath fed on choicer fare than we
May think to feed his throat with ere we die.

[Exeunt with the **BODY**.

The Vatican

ALEXANDER and **LUCREZIA**

ALEXANDER
The day burns high. Thou hast not seen them—thou?

LUCREZIA
My brethren, sire? Nay, not since yesternight.

ALEXANDER
The night is newly dead. Since yestereven?

LUCREZIA
Nor then. I saw them when we parted here
Last.

ALEXANDER
I believe thou liest not. Girl, the day
Looks pale before thy glory. Brow, cheek, eye,
Lips, throat, and bosom, thou dost overshine
All womanhood man ever worshipped. Once
I held thy mother fairest born of all
That ever turned old Rome to heaven. Thou hast read
Her golden Horace?

LUCREZIA
Else were I cast out
From all their choir who serve the Muses.

ALEXANDER
Ay.
'Fair mother's fairer daughter,' dost thou deem
That praise was ever merited as by thee?
I cannot.

LUCREZIA
I concern myself no whit
If so it were or were not.

ALEXANDER
Thou dost well.
Thou hast not seen, thou sayest, Francesco?

LUCREZIA
Nay—

Give me some reliquary to swear it on—
Some rosary—crucifix or amulet,
Sorcerous or sacred.

ALEXANDER
Never twins were born
More like than thou and he—nor lovelier: yet
No twins were ye.

LUCREZIA
What ails thy Holiness?

ALEXANDER
I am ill at ease: my heart is sick. Last night
No revel here was held, and yet the day
Strikes heavier on me wearier, body and soul,
Than though we had rioted out with raging mirth
The lifelong length of darkness.

LUCREZIA
Evil hours
Fret somewhiles all folk living; none sees why:
No child sleeps always all night long.

ALEXANDER
Wast thou
Wakeful? No trouble clung about thee? Nought
Made the air of night heavier with presage felt
As joy feels fear and withers? I am not
Afraid: methinks I am very fear itself.

[Enter an **OFFICER** of the household

OFFICER
His holiness be gracious towards me.

ALEXANDER
Speak.
Thy face is death's: let death upon thy lips
Live.

OFFICER
Sire, the humblest hireling knave in Rome—
A waterman that plies his craft all night—
Craves audience even of thee.

ALEXANDER
A Roman?

OFFICER
Nay.
Some outlander—some Greek—they call the knave
George the Slavonian.

ALEXANDER
They?

OFFICER
The fisherfolk
On Tiber.

ALEXANDER
Bid him in: bid God himself
Come in with doom upon me.

[Exit **OFFICER**.

Hear'st thou, child—
Daughter?

LUCREZIA
What horror hangs on thee?

ALEXANDER
Abide,
And thou shalt know as I know.

[Enter **GIORGIO SCHIAVONE**

Speak. I say,
Speak. What thou art I know: and what I am
Thou knowest—and yet thou knowest not.

GIORGIO
Holiest sire,
Last night I kept my boat on Tiber—Sire,
The thing I saw was nothing of my deed—
It shook me out of sleep to see it—Lord,
Have mercy: look not so upon me.

ALEXANDER
Dog,
Speak, while thy tongue is thine.

GIORGIO
Two men came down

And peered along the water-side: and two
Came after—men whose eyes raked all the night,
Searching the shore—I lay beneath my boat—
Beside it on the darkling side—and saw.
Then came a horseman—Sire, his horse was white—
The moonshine made his mane like dull white fire—
And on his crupper heavily hung a corpse,
Arms held from swaying on this side, legs on that,
I know not which on either—but the men
Held fast that held: and hard on Tiber side
They swung the crupper towards the water—sharp
And swift as man may steer a horse—and caught
And slung their dead into the stream: and he
Drifted, and caught the moon across his face
That shone like life against it: and the chief
Till then sat silent as the moon at watch,
And then bade hurl stones on the drifting dead
And sink him out of sight; and seeing this done,
Rode thence, and they strode after.

ALEXANDER
Man, and thou—
Thou?

GIORGIO
Sire, I set my heart again to sleep:
I turned and slept under my boatside.

ALEXANDER
Man—
Dog—devil, if this be truth, and if my fear
Lie not—how hadst thou heart to hold thy peace?
How comes it that the warders of the shore
Knew not of thee, while yet the crime was hot,
What crime had made night hell?

GIORGIO
A thousand times
I have seen such sights, but never till this hour
Seen him who cared to hear of them.

ALEXANDER
Till now,
Never. He looks in God's mute face and mine,
And says it. God be good to me! But God
Will not—or is not. Where is then thy dead,
Devil, called of God from hell to smite—to scourge—
Me?

GIORGIO
Sire, at hand I left him.

ALEXANDER
Stir not. Bid
Thy fellows bring my dead before me.

[Exit **OFFICER**.

Nay,
But mine it is not yet—it may not be
Mine—while it may not be, it is not. Child,
It shall not be thy brother. Pray no prayer.
Prayer never yet brought profit. Be not pale.
Fear strikes more deep into the fearful heart
The wound it heals not.

[Enter **OFFICERS** with the body of **FRANCESCO**

What is he they bring?
O God! Thou livest! And my child is dead!

[Falls.

SCENE IV

The Vatican

ALEXANDER and **CÆSAR**

ALEXANDER
Thou hast done this deed.

CÆSAR
Thou hast said it.

ALEXANDER
Dost thou think
To live, and look upon me?

CÆSAR
Some while yet.

ALEXANDER
I would there were a God—that he might hear.

CÆSAR
'Tis pity there should be—for thy sake—none.

ALEXANDER
Wilt thou slay me?

CÆSAR
Why?

ALEXANDER
Am not I thy sire?

CÆSAR
And Christendom's to boot.

ALEXANDER
I pray thee, man,
Slay me.

CÆSAR
And then myself? Thou art crazed, but I
Sane.

ALEXANDER
Art thou very flesh and blood?

CÆSAR
They say,
Thine.

ALEXANDER
If the heaven stand still and smite thee not,
There is no God indeed.

CÆSAR
Nor thou nor I
Know.

ALEXANDER
I could pray to God that God might be,
Were I but mad. Thou sayest I am mad: thou liest:
I do not pray.

CÆSAR
Most holiest father, no.
Thy brain is not so sick yet. Thou and God
Friends? Man, how long would God have let thee live—

Thee?

ALEXANDER
Long enough he hath kept me, to behold
His face as fire—if his it be—and earth
As hell—and thee, begotten of my loins,
Satan.

CÆSAR
The firstfruits of thy fatherhood
Were something less than Satan. Man of God,
Vaunt not thyself.

ALEXANDER
I would I had died in the womb.

CÆSAR
Thou shalt do better, dying in Peter's chair:
Thou shalt die famous.

ALEXANDER
Ay: no screen from that,
No shelter, no forgetfulness on earth.
We shall be famed for ever. Hell and night,
Cover me!

CÆSAR
Hast thou heard that prayers are heard?
Or hast thou known earth, for a man's cry's sake,
Cleave, and devour him?

ALEXANDER
I have done this thing.
Thou hast not done it: thy deed is none of thine:
Upon my hand, upon my head, the blood
Rests.

CÆSAR
Wilt thou sleep the worse for this next year?

ALEXANDER
I will not live a seven days' space beyond
This.

CÆSAR
Thou hast lived thy seven days' space in hell,
Father: they say thou hast fasted even from sleep.

ALEXANDER

Ay.

CÆSAR

What they say and what thou sayest I hold
False. Though thou hast wept as woman, howled as wolf,
Above our dead, thou art hale and whole. And now
Behoves thee rise again as Christ our God,
Vicarious Christ, and cast as flesh away
This grief from off thy godhead. I and thou,
One, will set hand as never God hath set
To the empire and the steerage of the world.
Do thou forget but him who is dead, and was
Nought, and bethink thee what a world to wield
The eternal God hath given into thine hands
Which daily mould him out of bread, and give
His kneaded flesh to feed on. Thou and I
Will make this rent and ruinous Italy
One. Ours it shall be, body and soul, and great
Above all power and glory given of God
To them that died to set thee where thou art—
Throned on the dust of Cæsar and of Christ,
Imperial. Earth shall quail again, and rise
Again the higher because she trembled. Rome
So bade it be: it was, and shall be.

ALEXANDER

Son,
Art thou my son?

CÆSAR

Whom should thy radiant Rose
Have found so fit to ingraff with, and bring forth
So strong a scion as I am?

ALEXANDER

By my faith—
Wherein, I know not—by my soul, if that
Be—I believe it. God forgot his doom
When he thou hast slain drew breath before thee

CÆSAR

God
Must needs forget—if God remember. Now
This thing thou hast loved, and I that swept him hence
Held never fit for hate of mine, is dead,
Wilt thou be one with me—one God? No less,
Lord Christ of Rome, thou wilt be.

ALEXANDER
Ay? The Dove?

CÆSAR
What dove, though lovelier than the swan that lured
Leda to love of God on earth, might match
Lucrezia?

ALEXANDER
None. Thou art subtle of soul and strong.
I would thou hadst spared him—couldst have spared him.

CÆSAR
Sire,
I would so too. Our sire, his sire and mine,
I slew not him for lust of slaying, or hate,
Or aught less like thy wiser spirit and mine.

ALEXANDER
Not for the dove's sake?

CÆSAR
Not for hate or love.
Death was the lot God bade him draw, if God
Be more than what we make him.

ALEXANDER
Bread and wine
Could hardly turn so bitter. Canst thou sleep?

CÆSAR
Dost thou not? Flesh must sleep to live. Am I
No son of thine?

ALEXANDER
I would I saw thine end,
And mine: and yet I would not.

CÆSAR
Sire, good night.

[Exeunt

Algernon Charles Swinburne was born at 7 Chester Street, Grosvenor Place, in London, on April 5th, 1837. He was the eldest of six children born to Captain Charles Henry Swinburne and Lady Jane Henrietta, daughter of the 3rd Earl of Ashburnham, a wealthy Northumbrian family.

Swinburne spent his early years at East Dene in Bonchurch, on the Isle of Wight. As a child, Swinburne was nervous and frail, but also imbued with a nervous energy and fearlessness almost to the point of recklessness.

He was schooled at Eton College from 1849 to 1853. It was here that he first began to write poetry. He excelled at languages and whilst still at Eton won first prizes in both French and Italian.

From Eton he moved to Oxford where he attended at Balliol College from 1856. Here he met friends to whom he became closely attached, among them Dante Gabriel Rossetti, William Morris and Edward Burne-Jones, who in 1857, were painting their Arthurian murals on the walls of the Oxford Union. At Oxford Swinburne was mentored by Benjamin Jowett, the master of Balliol College, who recognised his poetic talent and, intervening on his behalf, tried to keep him from being expelled when he celebrated the Italian patriot Orsini, and his failed attempt on the life of Napoleon III in 1858. Swinburne had to leave the Universcity for a few months due to this but returned in May, 1860 but never received a degree.

Summers were usually spent at Capheaton Hall in Northumberland, the house of his grandfather, Sir John Swinburne, 6th Baronet, who had a famous library and was himself President of the Literary and Philosophical Society in Newcastle upon Tyne.

Swinburne proudly considered himself a native of Northumberland and this is reflected in poems such as the intensely patriotic 'Northumberland' and 'Grace Darling'. He enjoyed riding across the moors and was, it was said, a daring horseman, as he moved 'through honeyed leagues of the northland border', as he remembered the Scottish border in his Recollections.

In the period from 1857 to 1860, Swinburne was one of a number of Pre-Raphaelite's who visited and became part of Lady Pauline Trevelyan's intellectual circle at Wallington Hall, a few miles west of Morpeth in Northumberland.

After leaving college, he moved to London and began his career in earnest as well as becoming a constant visitor to the Rossetti's house. To Rossetti Swinburne was his 'little Northumbrian friend', an affectionate reference to Swinburne's small stature—a mere five foot four. Whatever Swinburne lacked in height he made up for in poetic talent. However, with the burden of such great talent came the unveiling of a dark side that was to cause him pain and would, at times, threaten his very existence with all manner of self-inflicted pains through drink, drugs and sado-machoism.

In 1860 Swinburne published two verse dramas; The Queen Mother and Rosamond but it would not be until 1865 that Swinburne would achieve literary success with Atalanta in Calydon.

In 1861, Swinburne visited Menton on the French Riviera to recover from the effects of yet another period of excess use of alcohol, staying at the Villa Laurenti. From Menton, Swinburne then travelled on to Italy, where he journeyed widely.

After Elizabeth Rossetti's death from suicide in 1862, he and Rossetti moved to Tudor House at 16 Cheyne Walk in Chelsea. The stories that survive from his year with Rossetti are typical Swinburne. In one, Rossetti once had to tell him to keep down the noise — he and a boyfriend had been sliding naked down the bannisters and disturbing Rossetti's painting. He took a sardonic delight in what the critic and biographer, Cecil Lang, calls "Algernonic exaggeration": When people began to talk scathingly about his homosexuality and other sexual proclivities, he circulated a story that he had engaged in pederasty and bestiality with a monkey — and then eaten it. How many of the stories were true and how many invented is unclear. Oscar Wilde called him "a braggart in matters of vice, who had done everything he could to convince his fellow citizens of his homosexuality and bestiality without being in the slightest degree a homosexual or a bestialiser."

In December 1862, Swinburne accompanied Scott and his guests on a trip to Tynemouth. Scott writes in his memoirs that, as they walked by the sea, Swinburne declaimed the as yet unpublished 'Hymn to Proserpine' and 'Laus Veneris' in his lilting intonation, while the waves 'were running the whole length of the long level sands towards Cullercoats and sounding like far-off acclamations'.

Swinburne possessed a curious combination of frail health and strength. He was small and slightly built, but an excellent swimmer and the first to climb Culver Cliff on the Isle of Wight. He had an extremely excitable disposition: people who met him described him as a "demoniac boy" who would go skipping about the room declaiming poetry at the top of his voice. In this as in many things, moderation was not the standard for him. Excess was. Once or twice he had fits, thought to be epileptic, in public; but he made this condition much worse by drinking past excess to unconsciousness. More than once he was delivered to the door in the small of the night, dead drunk. Throughout the 1860s and '70s he rode an alcoholic cycle of dissolution, collapse, drying out at home in the country, then returning to London where he would begin the cycle all over again.

His mania for masochism, particularly flagellation, most probably started in early childhood at Eton and was encouraged by his later friendships with Richard Monckton Milnes (one of Tennyson's fellow Apostles), who introduced him to the works of the Marquis de Sade, and Richard Burton, the Victorian explorer and adventurer. Swinburne was an alcoholic and algolagniac (a desire for sexual gratification through inflicting pain on oneself or others; sadomasochism). He found life difficult, unfulfilling but still his poetic talents pushed to the fore.

Although Swinburne continued to publish some works in periodicals in 1865 he was granted recognition by both public and critics with Atalanta in Calydon written in the style of a classical Greek tragedy.

There followed "Laus Veneris" and Poems and Ballads (1866), with their sexually charged passages, absolutely decadent for polite Victorian society, which were attacked all the more violently as a result. The poems written in homage of Sappho of Lesbos such as "Anactoria" and "Sapphics" were especially savaged. The volume also contained poems such as "The Leper," "Laus Veneris," and "St Dorothy" which evoke both Swinburne's and a general Victorian fascination with the Middle Ages, and are explicitly mediaeval in style, tone and construction. With its publication came instant notoriety. He was now identified with indecent and decadent themes and the precept of art for art's sake.

Swinburne's meeting in 1867 with his long-time hero Mazzini, the Italian patriot living in England in exile, was the beginning of a poetical journey that now became more serious and more engaged with serious thought, initially leading to the political poems in the volume Songs Before Sunrise.

Also in 1867 he was introduced to Adah Isaacs Menken, the American actress, poet and circus rider, whose main fame seemed to be riding naked on a horse (in fact she wore tight nude coloured clothing) for her performance in the melodrama Mazeppa (itself based on a poem by Lord Byron). Although they had a short affair Adah's quote implies that Swinburne was not ready for a relationship that did not involve some self-sabotage; "I can't make him understand that biting's no use."

In 1879, with Swinburne nearly dead from alcoholism and dissolution, his legal advisor Theodore Watts-Dunton took him in, and was gradually successful in getting him to adapt to a healthier lifestyle. Swinburne lived the rest of his life at Watts-Dunton's house. He saw less and less of his old bohemian friends, who thought him a prisoner at The Pines, but his growing deafness also accounts for some of his decreased sociability. By now Swinburne was 42, and was moving from a young man of rebelliousness to a figure of social respectability. It was said of Watts-Dunton that he saved the man and killed the poet.

It is clear that Swinburne had an addictive personality, and clearly incapable of moderation in his pursuit of any chosen vices. This, of course, would both nourish and perhaps sabotage his poetic career. His poetry follows the somewhat clichéd pattern of early flourish and later decline; indeed some of the fresher pieces in the second and third series of Poems and Ballads (published in 1878 and 1889) were actually written during his days at Oxford. Nevertheless, his last collection, A Channel Passage, has some beautiful poems, including "The Lake of Gaube."

He is best remembered as the supreme technician in metre, with a versatility which exceeds even Tennyson's, but which lacks a corresponding emotional range. His obsessions are not widely enough shared; and if he cannot shock us by the strangeness of his desires nor the shrillness of his anti-theistical exclamations, often what remains is not enough to fully engage with the audience.

Swinburne is considered a poet of the decadent school, although he perhaps professed to more vice than he actually indulged in to advertise his deviance. Common gossip of the time reported that he also had a deep crush on the explorer Sir Richard Francis Burton, despite the fact that Swinburne himself abhorred travel. Fact and fiction are easily absorbed by the other so are difficult to untangle even now.

Many critics consider his mastery of vocabulary, rhyme and metre impressive, although he has also been criticised for his florid style and word choices that only fit the rhyme scheme rather than contributing to the meaning of the piece. A. E. Housman, although a critic, had great praise for his rhyming ability: to Swinburne the sonnet was child's play: the task of providing four rhymes was not hard enough, and he wrote long poems in which each stanza required eight or ten rhymes, and wrote them so that he never seemed to be saying anything for the rhyme's sake.

Throughout his career Swinburne published literary criticism of great worth. His deep knowledge of world literatures contributed to a critical style rich in quotation, allusion, and comparison. He is particularly noted for discerning studies of Elizabethan dramatists and of many English and French poets and novelists. As well he was a noted essayist and wrote two novels.

Swinburne was nominated for the Nobel Prize in Literature every year from 1903 to 1907 and then again in 1909.

H.P. Lovecraft, the master of the dark side and a decent poet himself, considered Swinburne "the only real poet in either England or America after the death of Mr. Edgar Allan Poe."

Swinburne was also responsible for devising a poetic form called the roundel, a variation of the French Rondeau form. In 1883 he published A Century of Roundels with several of the roundels dedicated to Dante's sister, the poet Christina Georgina Rossetti. Swinburne wrote to Edward Burne-Jones in 1883: "I have got a tiny new book of songs or songlets, in one form and all manner of metres ... just coming out, of which Miss Rossetti has accepted the dedication. I hope you and Georgie [his wife Georgiana] will find something to like among a hundred poems of nine lines each, twenty-four of which are about babies or small children".

Opinions of the Roundel poems move between those who find them captivating and brilliant, to others who find them merely clever and contrived. One of them, A Baby's Death, was set to music by the English composer Sir Edward Elgar as the song "Roundel: The little eyes that never knew Light".

After the first Poems and Ballads, Swinburne's later poetry was devoted more to philosophy and politics, including the unification of Italy, particularly in the volume Songs before Sunrise. He did not stop writing love poetry entirely, indeed it was only in 1882 that his great epic-length poem, Tristram of Lyonesse, was published, its contents lyrical rather than shocking. His versification, and especially his rhyming technique, remain of high quality to the end.

Algernon Charles Swinburne died of influenza, at the Pines in London on April 10th, 1909 at the age of 72. He was buried at St. Boniface Church, Bonchurch on the Isle of Wight.

Algernon Charles Swinburne – A Concise Bibliography

Verse Drama
The Queen Mother (1860)
Rosamond (1860)
Chastelard (1865)
Bothwell (1874)
Mary Stuart (1881)
Marino Faliero (1885)
Locrine (1887)
The Sisters (1892)
Rosamund, Queen of the Lombards (1899)

Poetry
Atalanta in Calydon (1865)*
Poems and Ballads (1866)
Songs Before Sunrise (1871)
Songs of Two Nations (1875)
Erechtheus (1876)*
Poems and Ballads, Second Series (1878)
Songs of the Springtides (1880)
Studies in Song (1880)
The Heptalogia, or the Seven against Sense. A Cap with Seven Bells (1880)
Tristram of Lyonesse (1882)
A Dark Month & Other Poems

A Century of Roundels (1883)
A Midsummer Holiday and Other Poems (1884)
Poems and Ballads, Third Series (1889)
Astrophel and Other Poems (1894)
The Tale of Balen (1896)
A Channel Passage and Other Poems (1904)

*Although formally tragedies, Atlanta in Calydon and Erechtheus are traditionally included with his poetry.

Criticism
William Blake: A Critical Essay (1868, new edition 1906)
Under the Microscope (1872)
George Chapman: A Critical Essay (1875)
Essays and Studies (1875)
A Note on Charlotte Brontë (1877)
A Study of Shakespeare (1880)
A Study of Victor Hugo (1886)
A Study of Ben Johnson (1889)
Studies in Prose and Poetry (1894)
The Age of Shakespeare (1908)
Shakespeare (1909)

Major Collections
The Poems of Algernon Charles Swinburne, 6 vols. 1904.
The Tragedies of Algernon Charles Swinburne, 5 vols. 1905.
The Complete Works of Algernon Charles Swinburne, 20 vols. Bonchurch Edition. 1925-7.
The Swinburne Letters, 6 vols. 1959-62.